NEW HAVEN FREE PUBLIC LIBRARY

3 5000 09553 9978

D1385133

MITCHELL LIBRARY
37 HARRISON STREET
NEW HAVEN, CT 06515

Mitchell Branch
Library
37 Harrison St.
New Haven, CT
06515

INVENTORS
and Discoveries

Jeanne Sturm

www.rourkepublishing.com

© 2012 Rourke Publishing LLC

All rights reserved. No part of this book may be reproduced or utilized in any form or by any means, electronic or mechanical including photocopying, recording, or by any information storage and retrieval system without permission in writing from the publisher.

www.rourkepublishing.com

PHOTO CREDITS: Cover: © Cenk Unver, Cammeraydave, Daniel Wiedemann, Eddie Toro, Christian Draghici, aleksandar valasevic; Title Page: © Rolffimages; Page 2: © itox; Page 5: © Ivankmit, William Michael Norton; Page 6: © Paprico, joaquin croxatto; Page 7: © Constance McGuire, sparkia; Page 8: © Baris Simsek, Jasony00, Luri, Uros Petrovic; Page 9: © Tt, Wouter van Caspel, Vclements; Page 10: © joaquin croxatto, Milosluz; Page 11: © Plastique1; Page 12: © Ferguswang, Iliyan Kirkov, jgroup; Page 13: © Vangelis, Wikipedia, subjug, Enrique Gomez, 350jb; Page 14: © Nataliia Fedori, by_nicholas, Wikipedia; Page 15: © by_nicholas, Nataliia Fedori, Wikipedia, Greg Nicholas, Library of Congress, Brian Sullivan; Page 16: © NASA, Mike Young, Leon Van Speybroeck, Greg Nicholas; Page 17: © J. Van Meurs, HadelProductions, NASA; Page 18: © NASA, Wikipedia, subjug; Page 19: © NASA, Wikipedia, subjug, Don Nichols; Page 20: © NASA, Wikipedia, subjug, Andrew Dunn; Page 21: © NASA, Associated Press; Page 22: © Library of Congress, Konstanttin; Page 23: © R. Gino Santa Maria, Vladislav Zitikis, Siloto, Konstanttin; Page 24: © Wikipedia, Konstanttin; Page 25: © Tr3gi, Konstanttin; Page 26: © Evert F. Baumgardner; Page 27: © subjub, Wikipedia: Moffett Studio, Danil Chepko; Page 28: © Michael Kurtz, Michaol Kowalski, Wikipedia; Page 29: © Danil Chepko; Page 30: © Wikipedia, World Economic Forum; Page 31: © Wikipedia, Wikipedia: Daderot, Wikipedia: DustyDingo; Page 32: © Kjunix, Veni Markovski, Wikipedia; Page 33, 39: © Wikipedia; Page 34: © Wikipedia, subjug, Michael Flippo; Page 35: © Eric Gevaert, Dmitry Ternovoy; Page 36: © Wikipedia: Bukvoed, Wikipedia, adventtr; Page 37: © adventtr; Page 38: © Julia Tsokur; Page 40: © kvkirillov; Page 41: © National Museum of Health and Medicine, Washington, D.C., USPTO; Page 43: © Wikipedia: Beo Beyond; Page 44: © Karimala; Page 45: © Interactive Institute Energy Design

Edited by Precious McKenzie

Cover design and page layout by Teri Intzegian

Library of Congress Cataloging-in-Publication Data

Sturm, Jeanne
 Inventors and Discoveries / Jeanne Sturm.
   p. cm. -- (Let's Explore Science)
 Includes bibliographical references and index.
 ISBN 978-1-61741-785-6 (hard cover) (alk. paper)
 ISBN 978-1-61741-987-4 (soft cover)
 Library of Congress Control Number: 2011924830

Rourke Publishing
Printed in the United States of America, North Mankato, Minnesota
060711
060711CL

RouRke PublisHing

www.rourkepublishing.com - rourke@rourkepublishing.com
Post Office Box 643328 Vero Beach, Florida 32964

Table of Contents

CHAPTER ONE

Discoveries and Inventions—Two That Got Us Started

Since our earliest days, mankind's desire to learn more about the world has led to important inventions and discoveries. In working to solve problems, understand ourselves and our universe, and make everyday life easier, we are motivated to search, study, and build.

Inventions and discoveries are not the same thing. Discoveries occur when people learn something new about the world that they didn't know before. An invention is a new device created by a person or by a group of people.

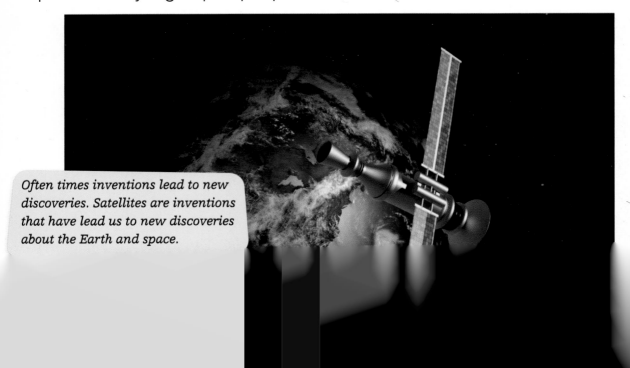

Often times inventions lead to new discoveries. Satellites are inventions that have lead us to new discoveries about the Earth and space.

Sometimes inventions are the brainchild of one person. More often, they are the result of many different people building on and adding to the developments of those who came before them. Sometimes they come in a flash, an "Aha" moment, but usually inventions are the result of trial and error. Success comes through determination and hard work.

Fire—
Now We're Cooking!

Fire has always been important to humans. We use it for warmth. We cook with it. Early humans, unable to make their own fire, noticed that lightning set fire to dry grass and brush. They learned to gather burning sticks and embers and use them to start their own campfires.

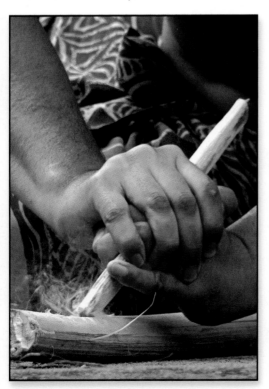

Men learned to make fire by rubbing two pieces of wood together.

Then people used wood to start fires. The larger piece of wood would have a small dip in the center. A person would set the larger piece on the ground and place dry grass in the dip. Then he would put one end of the second stick in the dip and rotate it rapidly between his palms. After awhile, the **friction** between the sticks would raise the temperature enough to **ignite** the dry grass.

Fire Plough Method

Circular motion creates friction.

Set bark beneath notch.

When early humans discovered how to start fire they also learned how to cook with fire.

Eventually, the invention of the bow drill made it easier and faster to start friction fires. Using a bow, a person could turn the wood more quickly and more steadily. He also had a free hand with which he could hold another piece of wood on top of the drill to exert downward force.

Lens Based Method

Others created sparks by striking **flint** against **pyrite**, then adding dry grass and twigs to get a fire going. Later, Greeks, Chinese, and other ancient civilizations learned to start fires using curved lenses. They held the lens in the sunlight and directed the Sun's rays onto kindling. Fire started quickly under the Sun's concentrated rays.

Flint and Steel Method

Flint   Pyrite

Bow and Drill Method

[A] Socket   [D] Bow

[B] Drill   [E] Cord

[C] Fireboard

In 1827, a man named John Walker invented friction matches, pieces of wood coated at one end with chemicals. Striking the match on a hard surface caused the chemicals to burst into flame. Now, disposable lighters provide instant fire at the flick of a thumb.

9

Where Would We Be without the Wheel and Axle?

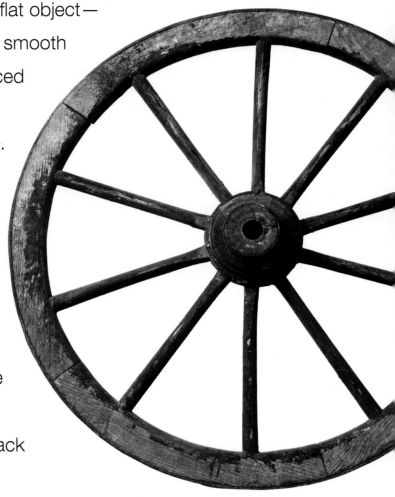

People started using wheels around 3500 BC. They started by using tree trunks as rollers. They would place a large, flat object— a sledge—on top of some smooth tree trunks. Then they placed the items they wanted to move on top of the sledge. It worked, but as they moved everything along, the sledge would eventually roll forward and off of the last tree trunk. To keep things advancing forward, people would have to continually pick up the tree trunk in back and move it to the front.

Wheels and axles made it much easier for people to haul materials and even farm.

When they used the same logs for a long time, the sledge began to wear away the wood under it, digging grooves into the logs. The deeper the grooves, the better it worked. People continued to improve the design. First, they added wooden pegs to the sledge to hold it in place on the thin part of the log. Later, they turned the thin part of the log into a true **axle** by attaching it to the sledge and letting it roll freely through holes in the wheels.

Windmill

Cranes

The wheel and axle made it possible to move heavy loads from place to place and they are essential in many items we now use every day, including bicycles, cars, trains, and scooters. They are necessary in an endless list of devices including faucets, pencil sharpeners, doorknobs, windmills, and many, many more. We use them in gears and pulleys. Without the wheel and axle, we would not be able to make clocks, motors, or even computers.

Early wheels were solid. Around 2000 BC, Egyptians began building chariots with spoked wheels. Large spoked wheels made it easy to travel quickly on uneven ground.

Bicycle

John Dunlop

Skateboard

In 1888, John Dunlop invented air-filled tires for bicycles, and in 1911, Philip Strauss developed an air-filled inner tube and tires for automobiles.

CHAPTER TWO

Higher and Faster— Inventions in Transportation

In 1783, Joseph and Jacques Montgolfier invented the hot-air balloon. The first flight, with a sheep, a duck, and a rooster aboard took to the air in September 1783. Two months later, two human passengers enjoyed a 23-minute flight over Paris, France.

In 1903, Orville and Wilbur Wright flew the first controlled flight in an airplane powered by a gasoline engine.

In 1913, automaker Henry Ford perfected the assembly line process of **mass production**.

1ʳᵉ EXPÉRIENCE AEROSTATIQUE A ANNONAY, le 4 Juin 1783

On June 4, 1783, the Montgolfier brothers demonstrate their balloon invention in Annonay, France. The balloon flies a little over one mile (2 kilometers) in about 10 minutes.

In an assembly line, a car moves along a track. As it passes each station, workers add a part to the car. This **innovation** reduced the time it took to assemble automobiles, from 728 minutes per car to just 93 minutes. After the invention of the assembly line, the Model T dropped in price from $850.00 to $300.00, making it affordable to not just the rich, but to ordinary people as well.

The Wright brothers' first flight happened on a beach in Kitty Hawk, North Carolina.

The efficient Ford assembly line inspired other companies to adopt the same process.

Although Ford cars have changed a lot since this 1932 model was made, the assembly line concept is much the same.

CHAPTER THREE

Discovering the Universe Around Us

There was a time when man knew little about our planet and our galaxy. Through study and the invention of telescopes, scientists learned about Earth and the other planets. They continue to search and study our solar system.

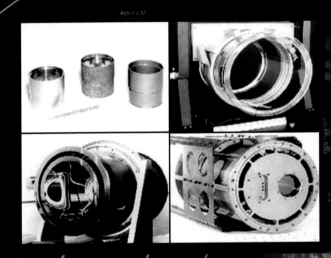

The Early Four

Discovery Timeline

384 BC

A

Aristotle, a Greek philosopher born in 384 BC, uses a geocentric model of the solar system to explain eclipses and the phases of the Moon. In a geocentric model, Earth is at the center of the solar system, with the Sun, Moon, stars, and known planets around it.

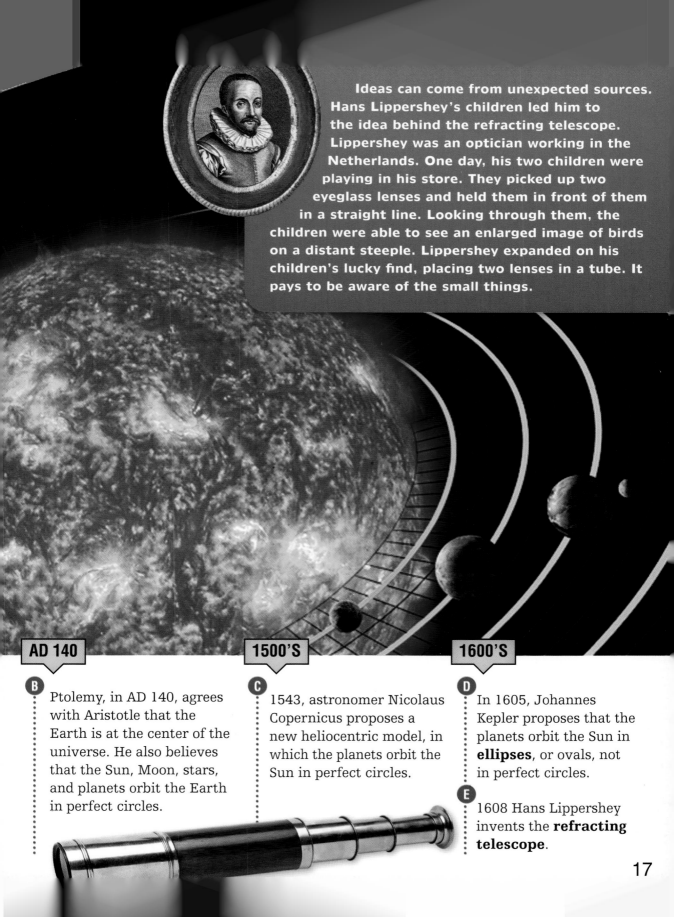

Ideas can come from unexpected sources. Hans Lippershey's children led him to the idea behind the refracting telescope. Lippershey was an optician working in the Netherlands. One day, his two children were playing in his store. They picked up two eyeglass lenses and held them in front of them in a straight line. Looking through them, the children were able to see an enlarged image of birds on a distant steeple. Lippershey expanded on his children's lucky find, placing two lenses in a tube. It pays to be aware of the small things.

AD 140

B Ptolemy, in AD 140, agrees with Aristotle that the Earth is at the center of the universe. He also believes that the Sun, Moon, stars, and planets orbit the Earth in perfect circles.

1500'S

C 1543, astronomer Nicolaus Copernicus proposes a new heliocentric model, in which the planets orbit the Sun in perfect circles.

1600'S

D In 1605, Johannes Kepler proposes that the planets orbit the Sun in **ellipses**, or ovals, not in perfect circles.

E 1608 Hans Lippershey invents the **refracting telescope**.

17

F 1609 Galileo builds a more powerful version of the refracting telescope. He discovers Jupiter's four largest moons and is able to describe our Moon's craters and Saturn's rings.

G 1668 Newton invents the **reflecting telescope**.

H 1660s-1670s As a professor of mathematics at Trinity College, Isaac Newton begins to study what happens when objects move. Newton's discoveries led him to develop his three laws of motion.

Galileo Galilei showing the Doge Dona how to use the telescope. Venice, Italy 1858

Isaac Newton

In 1687, Newton used his theory of gravity to explain how gravity holds planets in their orbits. Gravity is one of the key forces in the universe. It keeps the planets in orbit around the Sun and moons in orbit around their planets. Gravity is the force that causes things to fall to the Earth. The theory of gravity also states that every object in the universe exerts a gravitational force on every other object.

1770s-1780s William Herschel charts more than 800 double stars and 2,500 nebulae in the Milky Way Galaxy. Herschel discovers Uranus in 1781 and Saturn's sixth and seventh moons in 1789. His studies led him to the discovery that the Milky Way is a disk-shaped galaxy.

William Herschel

Scientists want to find out if life exists on other planets or in other galaxies.

1915-1919 Einstein develops his theory of general relativity. His theory proposes that **mass** warps both space and time. An experiment during a solar eclipse proves that the Sun's gravity bends light rays from distant stars.

Albert Einstein

K 1929 After using telescopes to explore galaxies beyond the Milky Way, astronomer Edwin Hubble concludes that the universe is expanding.

L 1977 Voyagers 1 and 2 launch from Kennedy Space Center in Florida. They explore Jupiter, Saturn, Uranus, and Neptune; then begin their Voyager Interstellar Mission (VIM) to explore the far reaches of the solar system and beyond.

Edwin Hubble used this telescope to measure galaxy redshifts and discover the general expansion of the universe.

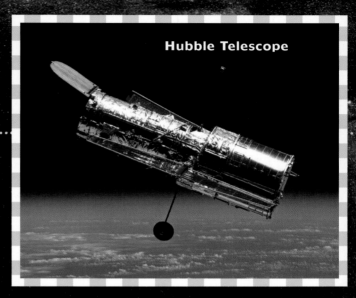

Hubble Telescope

M 1990 The United States launches the Hubble Space Telescope, named for Edwin Hubble. The telescope orbits about 350 miles (600 kilometers) above Earth. Two solar panels power the reflecting telescope as it looks far beyond the solar system to other galaxies.

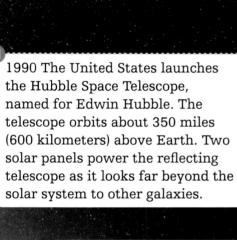

Kathryn Gray

{ In 2011, ten-year-old Kathryn Gray discovered a supernova in a galaxy 240 million light years away. Supernovas occur when stars far bigger than our Sun explode, sending out a bright light. They usually last for several weeks until they fade away. Kathryn's father, who assisted her in her find, had made six previous supernova discoveries, and family friend, David Lane, who photographed the image, had found three. Kathryn is the youngest person to discover a supernova. }

21

CHAPTER FOUR

Inventions Change the Way We Live

Some inventions have had a huge impact on the way people live their daily lives. Can you imagine how different your life would be without electric lights? Once the Sun went down, your only sources of light would be the fireplace, candles, or oil lamps.

Early oil lamps used olive, whale, or nut oil for fuel. They were smelly and smoky, and a gust of wind would blow them out. In the 1700s, people began using glass chimneys to protect the flame.

In 1792, William Murdoch discovered that gases from coal produced a steady, bright flame, and by the middle 1800s homes, businesses, and streetlights were using gas lamps. Gas wasn't perfect, though. It can be toxic to breathe, and it can explode. So inventors continued to search for a better solution.

Hot-Blast Kerosene Lantern

Air travels upwards and mixes with the gas. Many people used these lanterns indoors.

Swiss Kerosene Lantern

Knob adjusts the wick, and hence the flame size.

Traditional Karosene Lantern

It uses pressure and a mantle to adjust the flame. Many people still use kerosene lanterns as hurricane lanterns today.

Edison needed to find a filament that would burn for an extended period of time. He and his colleagues tried over 3,000 different approaches!

Thomas Edison joined the quest in 1878. His plan was to create a **filament** in a glass **vacuum** bulb. Edison made his own bulbs. His first **incandescent** light, developed in January 1879, worked, but its filament burned out after only a few short hours.

Edison's incandescent lamp worked by heating a strand of carbon until it was so hot that it glowed. Its glow was steady and bright, and it was far safer than the gaslight it replaced.

Traditional incandescent bulbs burn hotter and burn out more quickly than newer inventions.

The word incandescent means "to glow."

CFLs are new eco-friendly light bulbs.

At the same time, Sir Joseph Wilson Swan, a British inventor, invented an incandescent-filament electric lamp. Edison and Swan began working together. In 1880, they developed light bulbs that could burn for an extended time.

For years, incandescent light bulbs lit households around the world. Now, as we look for ways to reduce energy consumption, Americans are buying more Compact Fluorescent light bulbs (CFLs). Household CFLs use far less energy than incandescent bulbs, and they last much longer.

Televisions have had a huge impact on people's lives. In 1926, John Baird invented the Televisor, a machine that could scan and transmit moving images. In 1927, Philo Farnsworth **transmitted** a television image of a dollar sign made up of 60 horizontal lines. The United States began transmitting color images in 1951. The first satellite television stations began in 1989.

Many Americans did not have televisions in their homes in the 1950s. It was not unusual for friends and families to gather in the homes of those who owned a TV and watch a favorite show.

Alexander Graham Bell

Phones today do not have the rotary dial. You would place your finger in the circle for the number you wanted and rotate the dial. Today we use push buttons.

Alexander Graham Bell invented the first successful telephone in 1876. His first words spoken on the telephone were to his assistant, Thomas Watson. Bell was working on his invention when he spilled some chemicals on his clothes. He used his invention to call Watson, who was in another room, to come and help him.

In 1973, Dr. Martin Cooper of Motorola placed the first cell phone call on a phone about the size of a brick. He called his rival, the head of research at Bell Laboratories. In sharing the story 37 years later, Cooper recalled becoming so caught up in the phone call that he stepped into the street and was almost hit by a New York taxicab.

Early cell phones were very large and difficult to carry. Today's cell phones slip easily into small pockets.

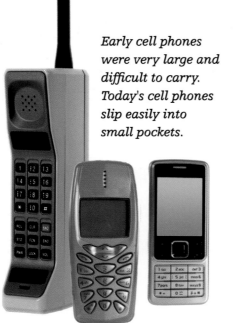

Many people prefer to text message one another rather than actually talk on the phone.

Neil Papworth sent the first text message in 1992. Papworth used a computer keyboard to type his message, Merry Christmas, and then sent it to a friend at a Christmas party. A few years later, cell phone manufacturers made cell phones that could send text easily.

CHAPTER FIVE

The Computer Age

As recently as 1970, you wouldn't find computers in people's homes. The first computers were about the size of a small room, and only large **corporations** and governments could afford them.

Bill Gates, 2007

Bill Gates believed that every office desk and every home should have a computer. Gates and Paul Allen, started a company called Microsoft to achieve that goal. In 1980, the IBM Corporation asked Gates and Allen to write software for personal computers they were developing.

Steve Jobs, 2007

Around the same time, Steve Jobs and Steve Wozniak formed the Apple Computer Company. They built personal computers that used a TV screen to display text, something most other computers did not have.

Steve Wozniak, 2005

COMPUTER TIMELINE

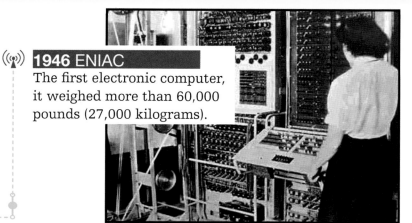

 1946 ENIAC
The first electronic computer, it weighed more than 60,000 pounds (27,000 kilograms).

Eniac

 1951 UNIVAC
UNIVAC is the first electronic computer to be produced for sale. The U.S. government used it to organize information collected in the 1950 census.

 1959 PDP-1
The first minicomputer, it sold for $120,000.

Univac 1

 1965 PDP-8
The first to use an **integrated circuit**, it sold for $20,000. It was small enough to fit on a desktop, making it popular in scientific laboratories.

 1971
Microprocessors made it possible to build much smaller computers.

31

Vint Cerf

Bob Kahn

 1973
Vint Cerf and Bob Kahn begin designing the Internet, a system that would allow computers to communicate with each other.

Apple Lisa

 1975 Altair 8800
The first mass-produced personal computer, the Altair was initially sold as a kit for $395.00. The user would have to build it before using it.

 1975
Bill Gates and Paul Allen start Microsoft.

1981
The first portable computer, the Osborne 1, sold for $1,795. It was the size of a small sewing machine and weighed 24 pounds (11 kilograms). It did not use a battery so users had to plug it in to use it.

 1983
The Apple Lisa was the first computer to use GUI (Graphical User Interface), making it much easier for those outside the scientific community to understand and use. It included a mouse and drop-down menus, as well as the ability to copy and paste information. It originally sold for $9,995.00.

Macintosh Portable

1989
Apple Computer released the Macintosh Portable, a laptop that later becomes the Powerbook.

Osborne 1

Computers continue to evolve. We use them to play games, research, shop, pay our bills, and connect with friends from around the world with just a couple of taps on the keyboard or touchscreen.

This NEXT Computer used by Tim Berners-Lee at CERN became the first web server.

 1990
Berners-Lee released the World Wide Web for public use through the Internet.

 1989
Tim Berners-Lee invents the World Wide Web to allow scientists to share their work with each other.

CHAPTER SIX

Creative Thinking Brings New Ideas

Not all inventions are as significant as the computer and the electric light bulb, but they still make our lives simpler or more fun. You probably never thought of the sandwich as an invention, but it is. One day in 1762, John Montagu was playing cards when he got hungry. He didn't want to stop playing, so he told his servants to put some meat between two pieces of bread and he ate it as he played. We call it a sandwich after his formal title, the Fourth Earl of Sandwich.

John Montagu

In 1904, at the World's Fair in St. Louis, Missouri, Arnold Fornachou was selling ice cream. He ran out of cups, but in the next booth, a baker was selling waffles. He rolled up a waffle to hold his ice cream and the waffle cone was born!

Sometimes, new discoveries are accidental. During World War II, British scientists invented the magnetron, a tube that produces short radio waves called microwaves. An American company called Raytheon found a way to mass-produce the magnetron. The British began using magnetrons in their shipboard radar systems to locate Nazi warplanes flying bombing raids from Germany.

Radar technology helps pilots fly airplanes and ship captains navigate the ocean.

The magnetron helped the Allied Forces defeat the Nazis in World War II.

Busy parents love microwave ovens because they can cook meals very quickly for their children.

A few years later, in 1945, Percy Spencer was standing in front of a magnetron tube when the candy bar in his pocket began to melt. Spencer, an engineer at Raytheon, placed some popcorn kernels in front of the tube, and they began popping. Next, he tried a raw egg, which exploded when the yolk cooked faster than the egg white. Spencer had discovered that the energy from microwave radio signals could cook food, and the microwave oven industry was born.

Sometimes a Difficult Process

It's not always easy to take an idea and turn it into a successful invention. Sometimes inventors run out of money before they finish developing their ideas. Others try different ideas without success. Sometimes two or more people are working on an invention at the same time. Each wants to finish first and patent his or her invention.

Women inventors faced **discrimination** from men. Before 1809, women could not even apply for a patent. African Americans also faced hurdles. Many could not get a good education and had to teach themselves. Yet, many succeeded.

Mary Kies became the first woman to receive a U.S. Patent for her method of weaving straw with silk.

What is a Patent?

• A U.S. patent grants property rights to the inventor. That means that the invention belongs to the inventor and no one else can make, use, or sell the invention in the United States without permission. Nor can anyone bring the invention into the United States from another country.

• Sometimes people improve upon existing inventions. They can file a patent on their improved design, but if the original product is still under patent, then they must get permission from the original patent holder.

• In the United States, most new patents protect the product for 14 or 20 years, depending on the type of invention. Once the patent expires, anyone can make, use, or sell the product without permission from the patent holder.

Concept • Invention • Innovation

PATENT PROCESS

Patent Disclosure

Evaluation

Written Estimate Generated

Estimate Application

Funds Deposited in Client's Trust Account

Firm Completes Patent Application Draft

Client Approves Draft

Patent is Filed with United States Patent and Trademark Office

Sarah Goode was one of these women. Goode owned a furniture store in Chicago, Illinois. She noticed that many people who lived in apartments had little space for furniture so she invented a desk that unfolded into a bed. She called it the Cabinet Bed. When closed, it was a working desk. When nighttime came, the owner would open it up to reveal the bed. Goode, who had been born into slavery in 1850, grew up to become the first African American woman to receive a patent.

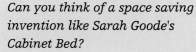

Can you think of a space saving invention like Sarah Goode's Cabinet Bed?

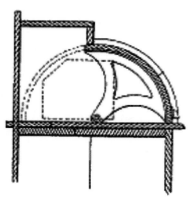

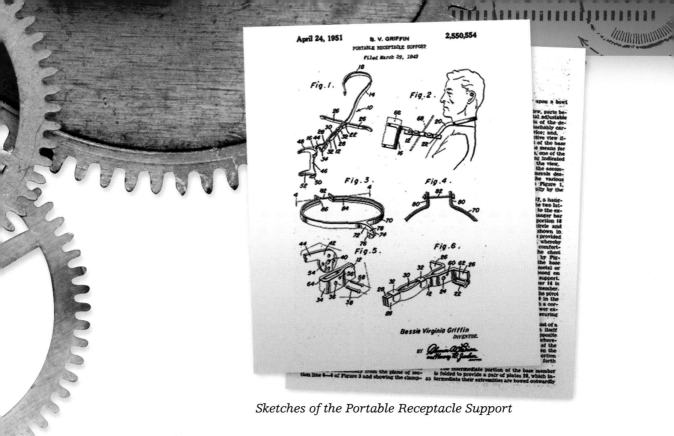

Sketches of the Portable Receptacle Support

Bessie Blount Griffin, born in 1914, was a physical therapist, inventor, and forensic scientist. During World War II, Griffin worked with injured soldiers. Many of the men had sustained injuries that left them unable to feed themselves.

In 1951, Griffin invented an electronic feeding device. Food traveled to the patient's mouth through a tube. The patient could control how much food he ate by biting down on the tube.

Griffin also invented a device that patients could wear around their necks in which to hold food, drink, or other small items. She named it the Portable Receptacle Support and received a U.S. patent for it. Both of Griffin's inventions helped injured people regain some of their independence.

CHAPTER SEVEN

What Can You Invent?

Do you have an idea that would make a great invention? You'd be in good company. Many useful inventions have come from kids.

In the early 1970s, 10 year-old Becky Schroeder waited in the car as her mother finished shopping. Becky wanted to work on her math homework, but it was getting dark out and she couldn't see. She realized that if she had paper that could light up, she would be able to see to do her work. That's when Becky decided to invent paper that glowed.

She thought of the Frisbees she had that glowed in the dark, and learned that phosphorescence made them glow. Becky bought phosphorescent paint and used it to paint stacks of paper. It worked! The paper glowed in the dark.

Then Becky realized it was the clipboard, not the paper, that needed to glow. She painted her clipboard with phosphorescent paint and, sure enough, it was bright enough to shine through a piece of paper clipped to it. Becky continued to improve her glow-in-the-dark clipboard. She added batteries to produce a steady glow.

Artists experiment with new technologies in order to awe and inspire their audiences.

The New York Times wrote a story about Becky's invention, and people started buying them. Emergency medical technicians used them in ambulances. Photographers used them to write things down as they developed photographs in their darkrooms. Doctors used them in hospital rooms at night so they wouldn't disturb their patients by turning on the light. Even NASA and the U.S. Navy were interested in Becky's invention.

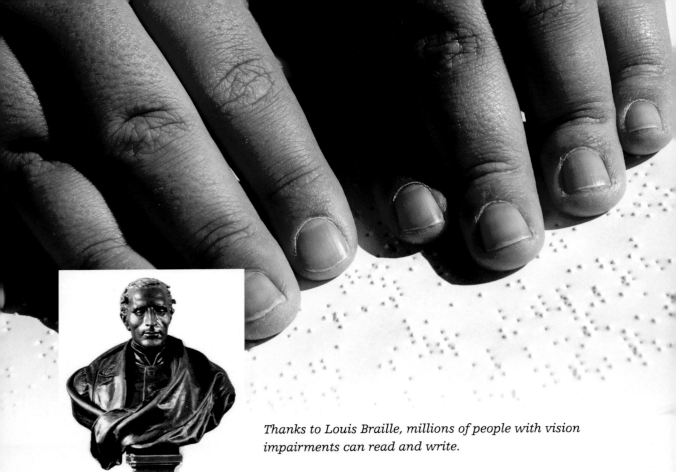

Thanks to Louis Braille, millions of people with vision impairments can read and write.

Louis Braille was injured and lost his sight at three years of age. In 1824, at age 15, Louis was a student at the Royal Institute for Blind Youth in Paris, France. Louis wanted to be able to read and write, so he developed a system of raised dots imprinted on paper. His system, called Braille, is still in use today.

New ideas are always on the horizon. Engineers have developed a plastic device filled with water and explosives. Kind of like a pumped-up squirt gun, the device generates a thin blade of water that can cut through a bomb's metal walls. In war torn areas, soldiers can use the device to disable and destroy roadside bombs before the bombs can harm troops or civilians.

Inventions can make the world a safer place or teach us to use less electricity. We can use them to solve problems in our own lives or to make recreation more fun. Is there a job you'd like to make more simple? Maybe you can be the next great inventor!

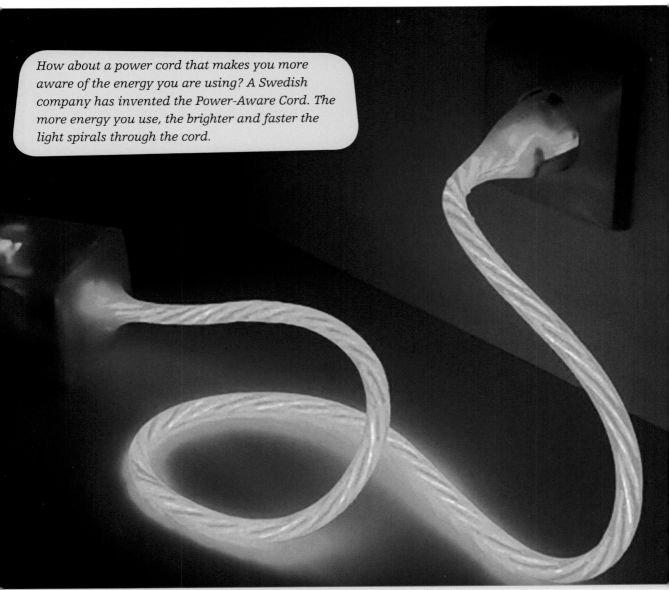

How about a power cord that makes you more aware of the energy you are using? A Swedish company has invented the Power-Aware Cord. The more energy you use, the brighter and faster the light spirals through the cord.

Glossary

axle (AK-suhl): the rod on which a wheel turns

corporations (kor-puh-RAY-shuhnz): companies run by groups of people

discrimination (diss-krim-i-NAY-shuhn): unfair treatment of others because they are a different age, race, or gender

ellipses (i-LIP-seez): oval shapes

filament (FIL-uh-muhnt): a thin thread of tungsten that glows and lights up

flint (FLINT): a hard stone that produces sparks when struck by steel

friction (FRIK-shuhn): heat caused by rubbing

ignite (ig-NITE): to set something on fire

incandescent (in-kan-DESS-uhnt): glowing with great light and heat

innovation (in-uh-VAY-shuhn): a new invention or a new way to use an existing invention

integrated circuit (IN-tuh-gray-tuhd SUR-kit): a set of electronic parts imprinted on a tiny chip

mass (MASS): the amount of matter in an object

mass production (MASS pruh-DUHK-shuhn): making large quantities of something on an assembly line

pyrite (PYE-rite): a mineral that produces sparks when hit by metal or another mineral

reflecting telescope (ri-FLEKT-ing TEL-uh-skope): a telescope that uses a single mirror or combination of mirrors

refracting telescope (ri-FRAKT-ing TEL-uh-skope): a telescope that uses a lens to bring distant images into focus

transmitted (transs-MIT-ing): sent

vacuum (VAK-yoom): a sealed area or object with no air or gas inside

Index

Wesites to Visit

www.inventors.about.com/od/astartinventions/a/FamousInvention.htm

www.nasm.si.edu/wrightbrothers/

www.inventored.org/k-12/

www.women-inventors.com/

www.thocp.net/

About the Author

Jeanne Sturm grew up exploring the woods, waterfalls, and riverbanks around her home in Chagrin Falls, Ohio. She earned her Education degree at Bowling Green State University and moved to Tampa, Florida, to teach. She began windsurfing, where she met her future husband. Now married, Jeanne, her husband, and their three children live in Land O' Lakes, Florida, with their dog, Astro.

MAR   2012| NEW HAVEN FREE PUBLIC LIBRARY